Contents

KU-754-819

Any words appearing in the text in bold, **like this**, are explained in the glossary. You can also look out for them in the Word bank at the bottom of each page.

Non-metals everywhere

Gases in air

The air is made of pure non-metals and non-metals that have combined with each other. The **composition** of air is:

- 78% nitrogen
- 21% oxygen
- 0.9% argon
- 0.1% carbon dioxide, neon, helium, krypton, water vapour and other gases.

- ▢ nitrogen
- ▢ oxygen
- ▢ argon
- ▢ carbon dioxide, neon, helium, krypton, water vapour and other gases

This chart shows the proportion of different non-metals in air.

As people hike in the hills, the air is clear, cool and crisp. When they take a deep breath of air, their lungs fill with a **mixture** of non-metals. Then they look down at the city in the valley far below. Why does the air down there look brownish instead of clear and colourless? More non-metals are to blame. So, what exactly makes up air?

Gases

Air is a mixture of gases. All the gases in air belong to a group called non-metals. But not all non-metals are gases. A few are solids and one is a liquid at room temperature.

Many non-metals are present in the air we breathe. In cities like Los Angeles, they can form **smog**.

>>>>>>>>>>>>>>>>>>>>>>>>

Turn to page 26 to find out which non-metals cause the brownish haze seen over some cities.

Word bank composition materials that make up a substance

Non-metals in us

The human body is mostly made of non-metals. About 65 per cent of a person's body weight is made of the non-metal oxygen. Carbon, another non-metal, makes up 18 per cent of the body. Hydrogen makes up 10 per cent and nitrogen makes up 3 per cent. Metals, such as calcium, and non-metals such as phosphorus, sulphur, chlorine and iodine make up the other 4 per cent.

Fast fact
Other animals' bodies have different amounts of non-metals in them. For example, some jellyfish are 95 per cent hydrogen and oxygen, in the form of water.

Find out later...

What non-metal is used as rocket fuel?

What non-metal is made by plants?

How can you be sure a dangerous non-metal is not lurking in your home?

mixture   materials combined physically but not chemically
smog   fog caused by smoke and other pollutants

Properties of non-metals

Discovering chlorine

In 1774, the Swedish chemist Carl Wilhelm Scheele put a few drops of hydrochloric acid on a piece of manganese dioxide. Within seconds a greenish-yellow gas was given off. He had no idea at the time, but he had just discovered the non-metal chlorine.

Non-metals can be solids, liquids or gases. Most are gases at room temperature. The non-metal gases are:

- hydrogen
- helium
- nitrogen
- oxygen
- fluorine
- chlorine
- neon
- argon
- krypton
- xenon
- radon

The following non-metals are solids at room temperature:

- carbon
- phosphorus
- sulphur
- iodine
- astatine

Bromine is the only non-metal that is a liquid at room temperature.

Some non-metals are opaque

Most solids are **opaque**. That means we cannot see light through them. They completely block the light and cause shadows. All metals are opaque. Most non-metals that are solids are opaque too. We cannot see light passing through a piece of sulphur. Light does not pass through the **graphite** in pencils, either.

Chlorine is a gas at room temperature.

Fast fact
Table salt that we put on our food is a **compound** of the metal sodium and the non-metal chlorine.

Turn to page 37 to find out about the uses of chlorine.

Word bank   graphite   a form of carbon, used in pencils
opaque   (oh PAYK) not letting light pass through

Some non-metals are transparent or translucent

Many liquids are **translucent**. They stop some, but not all, light from passing through them. Diamond is a solid translucent non-metal. **Transparent** substances let light pass right through them. A liquid is translucent or transparent depending on its thickness. Light can pass through a thin layer of water. But it cannot pass through a thick layer of water. That is why the deepest parts of the ocean are pitch black. Bromine is similar. Light can pass through a bottle of bromine, but not through a large tank of bromine. Gases are usually transparent. We can see through clean air because it is made of transparent gases.

Turn to page 40 to learn how divers avoid the bends.

The iodine in this dish is a greyish-purple solid. It gives off violet iodine vapour as it is heated.

Dangerous nitrogen

People breathe in nitrogen in air without a problem. However, nitrogen can cause problems for scuba divers who dive too deep for too long. Nitrogen bubbles form in the body if the diver surfaces too quickly. These bubbles can cause pain, dizziness, loss of feeling or even death. This is called 'the bends'.

---

translucent   stopping some, but not all, light from passing through
transparent   letting light pass through

Densities of some non-metals

Metals have very high densities compared to non-metals. The density of iron is 7.87 grams per cubic centimetre. The metal osmium is three times as dense as this. Even a light metal like aluminium, used to make drinks cans, has a density of 2.7 grams per cubic centimetre. Compare this to the densities of some non-metals in the table below.

Non-metals have low densities

Density is a measure of how much **mass** is contained in a certain **volume** of matter, or how many particles of matter are packed into a certain amount of something. You can find the density of something by dividing its mass by its volume. Mass is measured in grams or kilograms. Volume is measured in cubic centimetres or cubic metres. For example, 2 cubic centimetres of lead has a mass of 22.8 grams. So dividing 22.8 grams (mass) by 2 cubic centimetres (volume) gives you a density of 11.4 grams per cubic centimetre.

Non-metals have lower densities than metals. Carbon's low density is one reason why carbon fibres are used in lightweight fishing rods. The non-metal gases have very low densities. Helium has a lower density than oxygen and nitrogen in air. Helium-filled balloons will float upwards in the air.

The low density of helium is the reason it is used to fill the bags of airships.

Non-metal	Density (grams per cubic centimetre)
Hydrogen	0.00009
Helium	0.000179
Oxygen	0.00143
Nitrogen	0.00125
Argon	0.00178
Radon	0.00973
Chlorine	0.00321
Phosphorus	1.82
Sulphur	2.07
Carbon	2.27
Bromine	3.2

Word bank   atoms   particles that make up all substances
compound   substance made of different kinds of atom joined together

Forming compounds

Non-metals can join with other non-metals or metals to form **compounds**. For example, water is a compound of two non-metals. Hydrogen and oxygen join to form water. Carbon dioxide gas in air is another compound. It is made of carbon and oxygen that have joined together. Sugar is a compound made of carbon, hydrogen and oxygen.

Non-metals also join with metals like copper, sodium and iron. Common table salt is a compound of sodium and chlorine. Rust on an old car is a compound of iron and oxygen. Copper, sulphur and oxygen form the green compound that coats the Statue of Liberty.

Diatomic gases

Like all materials, non-metals are made of tiny particles called **atoms**. Some non-metal atoms join in pairs. They form what we call **diatomic** gases. Diatomic means 'two atoms'. Hydrogen, nitrogen, chlorine and fluorine are also diatomic gases.

In this diagram, the black bar represents the strong bond between the two hydrogen atoms.

➤ ➤ ➤ ➤ ➤ ➤ ➤

Turn to page 12 to learn more about atoms.

An air-filled object can float on water because of the low densities of gases in air.

density   mass of a certain volume of something; measured in grams per cubic centimetre or kilograms per cubic metre

Non-metals are brittle

Metals are **malleable**. That means they can be easily bent or formed into a new shape. Metals are also **ductile**. That means they can be stretched to form wires. Non-metals are neither malleable nor ductile. All solid non-metals are **brittle**. That means they will break rather than bend or stretch. **Graphite**, the form of carbon used in pencils, is brittle. We can tell that it is brittle because pencil points often break. Diamond, the form of carbon used in jewellery, will shatter when it is hit hard.

Non-metals are not shiny

Solid non-metals do not have a metallic **lustre** either. That means they do not shine like the polished surface of a metal such as gold. Solid non-metals usually look dull like graphite.

Malleable metals like silver can be hammered or shaped without breaking.

brittle   having a firm texture but easily broken
conductor   material through which heat or electricity pass easily

Non-metals are poor conductors

Unlike metals, non-metals are not good **conductors** of heat. That means heat does not travel quickly or easily through them. Things that are poor conductors of heat are usually said to be good **insulators**. Air is a good insulator. Birds fluff up their feathers in cold weather. This traps air between their feathers and helps keep them warm. People also wear down jackets because air trapped between the down feathers is a good insulator.

Non-metals, except for graphite, are also good insulators and poor conductors of electricity. In winter, dry indoor air is a good insulator. If you walk across a carpet, your body builds up an electric charge because the static electricity created as you walk cannot escape through the non-metal air or carpet. Only when you touch something metal, like a doorknob, can the electric charge flow off your body. You might feel a small electric shock as this happens.

Phosphorus versus copper

Unlike the non-metal phosphorus, the metal copper is a good conductor of electricity. Unlike phosphorus, copper is also a good conductor of heat. Because of this, many cooking pans have copper bottoms.

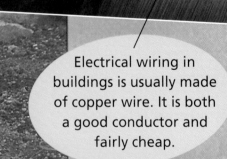

Like other solid non-metals, sulphur is brittle.

Electrical wiring in buildings is usually made of copper wire. It is both a good conductor and fairly cheap.

---

ductile   able to be drawn into a wire
insulator   material through which heat or electricity do not pass easily

11

The periodic table

The heads of these matches contain the non-metal phosphorus. The chemical symbol for phosphorus is P.

Symbols of elements

Chemical symbols are a short way of writing the names of the elements. Symbols are either one or two letters, and the first is always a capital letter. Some symbols are the first letter or first two letters of an element's name. Other elements have two-letter symbols that are not the first two letters of their names.

Atoms and ions

Matter can be broken down into very tiny bits called **atoms**. Most of the **mass** of an atom is in its **nucleus**. This centre part of the atom is made of two kinds of particles. **Protons** are particles with a tiny positive electric charge. **Neutrons** are particles that are neutral, or have no charge.

Electrons are particles with a tiny negative electric charge. In an atom, the number of electrons is the same as the number of protons. Their electrical charges balance. So the atom is neutral. Sometimes, however, atoms can gain or lose one or more electrons. Then they become **ions**. Ions have either extra positive or extra negative electric charges.

Key

- ☐ metals
- ▨ metalloids
- ▨ non-metals

Example

2 — group number
beryllium — name
Be — symbol

1	2							
hydrogen **H**								
lithium **Li**	beryllium **Be**							
sodium **Na**	magnesium **Mg**		The Transition Metals					
potassium **K**	calcium **Ca**	scandium **Sc**	titanium **Ti**	vanadium **V**	chromium **Cr**	manganese **Mn**	iron **Fe**	cobalt **Co**
rubidium **Rb**	strontium **Sr**	yttrium **Y**	zirconium **Zr**	niobium **Nb**	molybdenum **Mo**	technetium **Tc**	ruthenium **Ru**	rhodium **Rh**
caesium **Cs**	barium **Ba**		hafnium **Hf**	tantalum **Ta**	tungsten **W**	rhenium **Re**	osmium **Os**	iridium **Ir**
francium **Fr**	radium **Ra**		rutherfordium **Rf**	dubnium **Db**	seaborgium **Sg**	bohrium **Bh**	hassium **Hs**	meitnerium **Mt**

Word bank   element   substance made of only one kind of atom
ion   atom or group of atoms that has an electric charge

Elements

Not all atoms have the same number of protons, neutrons and electrons. Over a hundred different kinds of atoms have been discovered. Each kind of atom is an **element**. An atom is the basic unit of an element. Sometimes different kinds of elements join together to form a **compound**. Sand is a compound of the elements silicon and oxygen.

Grouping elements

Elements are grouped in a chart called the **periodic table**. The vertical columns are called groups. All elements in a group have similar properties because their electrons are arranged in similar patterns. A stepped line in the table separates the metals from the other elements. Except for hydrogen, all the non-metals are on the right-hand side of the periodic table.

Metalloids

Some elements are neither metals nor non-metals. These elements are called **metalloids**. They have properties of both metals and non-metals. Silicon and arsenic are examples of metalloids. They are both used in computer chips and solar cells.

						0
						helium
						He
3	4	5	6	7		
boron	carbon	nitrogen	oxygen	fluorine	neon	
B	**C**	**N**	**O**	**F**	**Ne**	
aluminium	silicon	phosphorus	sulphur	chlorine	argon	
Al	**Si**	**P**	**S**	**Cl**	**Ar**	

nickel	copper	zinc	gallium	germanium	arsenic	selenium	bromine	krypton
Ni	**Cu**	**Zn**	**Ga**	**Ge**	**As**	**Se**	**Br**	**Kr**
palladium	silver	cadmium	indium	tin	antimony	tellunum	iodine	xenon
Pd	**Ag**	**Cd**	**In**	**Sn**	**Sb**	**Te**	**I**	**Xe**
platinum	gold	mercury	thallium	lead	bismuth	polonium	astatine	radon
Pt	**Au**	**Hg**	**Tl**	**Pb**	**Bi**	**Po**	**At**	**Rn**
ununnilium	unununium	ununbium		ununquadium				
Uun	**Uuu**	**Uub**		**Uuq**				

Silicon chips are now so small an ant can carry one. Metalloids are used in computer chips because they conduct electricity in special ways.

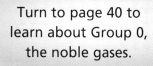

Turn to page 40 to learn about Group 0, the noble gases.

---

metalloids elements that have properties of both metals and non-metals
nucleus dense, positively charged centre of an atom

Hydrogen

Hydrogen in the Earth's atmosphere

There is very little hydrogen gas in the Earth's **atmosphere**. Suppose you had 100 million litres of air. Of that air, only about 5 litres would be hydrogen. That is a very small amount when you think about how much of the universe is made of hydrogen.

Hydrogen is the simplest of all the **atoms**. It is made of a single **proton,** circled by a single electron. Hydrogen is the most common **element** in the universe. It is the main element found in all stars. Huge amounts of hydrogen also exist in space between the stars. About 930 out of every 1000 atoms in the universe are hydrogen atoms. About 69 out of every 1000 atoms are helium atoms. Atoms of all the other elements make up the remaining 0.1 per cent. Because there are too many atoms in the universe to even begin to count, there are still plenty of atoms of all the other elements.

Air contains just 0.000005 per cent hydrogen, but 93 per cent of atoms in the universe are hydrogen.

At its centre, the Sun changes hydrogen to helium at a rate of 700 million tonnes every second.

Word bank   atmosphere   layer of gases that surrounds the Earth
flammable   easily set on fire

Hydrogen gas

Hydrogen gas is a diatomic gas made of two atoms of hydrogen joined together. The symbol for the gas is written as H_2 to show that the two atoms are joined. Hydrogen gas has no **odour** or taste and is completely colourless. That means you really cannot tell when it is present. Hydrogen has the lowest density of any gas. People often say this means that hydrogen is lighter than air. A balloon filled with hydrogen will rise and float away when it is released.

However, hydrogen is a very **flammable** gas. When hydrogen burns, it joins with oxygen very quickly, releasing huge amounts of heat.

Hydrogen disaster

Hydrogen's low density gives it great lifting power. The gas was once used in airships. As the large airship *Hindenburg* tried to land in New Jersey in 1937, a spark ignited the hydrogen inside it. The airship burst into flames and crashed.

After the *Hindenburg* accident, hydrogen was no longer used in airships.

odour smell

15

Car batteries

Sometimes a car battery goes 'dead' and the car will not start. People often recharge the battery so it will work again but they have to be careful. The battery contains a strong acid. Recharging it produces hydrogen gas. A spark or flame near the battery can make it explode.

Extracting hydrogen from acids

Acids such as vinegar, hydrochloric acid and sulphuric acid contain hydrogen. A **chemical reaction** can be used to produce hydrogen gas from an acid. One way to produce hydrogen gas is the reaction between an acid and a metal. In 1766, the English chemist Henry Cavendish produced hydrogen gas by adding some zinc metal to an acid. This method is still used to make small amounts of hydrogen gas in labs. A **mixture** of hydrogen and air in a test tube produces a small explosion when brought near a flame.

Fast fact
To test for hydrogen in the lab, a lighted splint is held in the mouth of a test tube of the gas. The burning splint makes hydrogen pop.

To be safe, a car battery should be recharged in a place with plenty of fresh air.

Word bank   chemical reaction   change that produces one or more new substances
coke   form of carbon made from coal

Hydrogen and water

On the Earth, the most common **compound** of hydrogen is water. When water forms, two atoms of hydrogen join with one **atom** of oxygen. So the chemical formula for water is H_2O. Water is used to produce large amounts of hydrogen gas.

Hydrogen is usually made by breaking water apart. Steam is passed over hot carbon in the form of **coke**. The steam reacts with the coke to produce **carbon monoxide** and hydrogen gases. These two gases can easily be separated. Sometimes, however, the two gases are left mixed together. This mixture is used as a **fuel** by industry and is called 'water gas'. Both hydrogen and water gas are **compressed** and stored in cylinders.

The 'water gas reaction' can produce large amounts of hydrogen gas. Hydrogen is used to make fertilizers, rocket fuel and hydrochloric acid.

Water maker

The reaction of hydrogen and oxygen to form water gave hydrogen its name. The name comes from the Greek words *hydro*, meaning 'water' and *genes*, meaning 'forming'. The German word for hydrogen is *wasserstoff*, meaning 'water stuff'.

---

compressed   squeezed into a smaller space
fuel   any material that can be burned to produce useful heat or power

Hydrogen can be extracted from coal, but this is not good for the environment.

Hydrogen compounds

Hydrogen joins with carbon and oxygen to form many compounds. These include sugars, starches, fats and proteins. These compounds are found in all living things. Hydrogen is also found in coal, natural gas and crude oil products such as petrol and paraffin.

Large amounts of liquid hydrogen are used in rockets that allow the space shuttle to blast into space.

Word bank cholesterol   fatty substance in some foods that can clog blood vessels
dissolve   mix completely and evenly

Hydrogen is used to make ammonia

Large amounts of hydrogen are used to make ammonia. Ammonia, NH_3, is a colourless gas with a strong odour. It is a **compound** of nitrogen and hydrogen. It **dissolves** easily in water and is used in many household cleaning products. Ammonia is also used to make **fertilizers** for growing crops.

Hydrogen is used to get metals

Many metals that we use are found combined with oxygen. These compounds are called oxides. The metals have to be separated from the oxygen before we can use them. One way of doing this is by using hydrogen. For example, hydrogen will react with copper oxide to produce copper and water. The same process can be used to get silver and iron metals.

Hydrogen is used in foods

Vegetable oils, such as peanut oil and coconut oil, are liquids. Vegetable oil is often treated with hydrogen. During this process the oil changes to a solid, such as margarine. Margarine contains less **cholesterol** than butter. Cholesterol is a fatty substance that can clog blood vessels. So many people use margarine as a substitute for butter.

Hydrogen is used as rocket fuel

Liquid hydrogen is an important rocket **fuel**. The main engines of the space shuttle use liquid hydrogen and liquid oxygen in two separate tanks. The hydrogen and oxygen are pumped together. Hydrogen burns in oxygen to produce hot steam. The steam rushes out of openings in the bottom of the engines. This pushes the shuttle upwards.

Pure power

Hydrogen is being studied as a fuel for cars, trucks and buses. When hydrogen and oxygen are combined to make water, electricity can be produced. That is what a hydrogen fuel cell does. The electricity runs the car's motor.

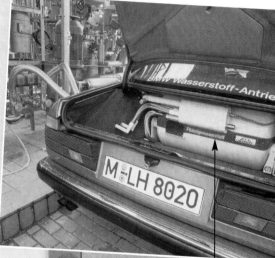

In a car with a hydrogen fuel cell, the only thing that comes from the car's exhaust pipe is water vapour. That means the car does not add **pollution** to the air.

fertilizer   chemicals added to soil to help plants grow better
pollution   harmful things in the air, water or land

19

Carbon

Carbon is found in different forms and in many different **compounds**. It is in the food you eat and the clothes you wear. It is also found in your pencils and in expensive jewellery.

Diamond

One form of carbon is diamond. In diamond, the carbon **atoms** are packed in a tight, repeating pattern. Each carbon atom is joined to four others. Diamond has a high density and is very hard. In fact, diamond is the hardest substance known. But diamond is also very **brittle**. It will shatter if hit with a hammer.

Most diamonds are colourless, but they can be blue, pink, yellow or other colours. Coloured diamonds are rare and often very valuable. The best diamonds are used in jewellery. Other diamonds are used for cutting and grinding.

This is a magnified photo of a drill covered in **synthetic** diamonds. These are used by dentists. The diamond fragments are hard enough to cut through teeth.

Synthetic diamonds

Diamonds can be made from graphite. This is done by heating graphite to very high temperatures under very high pressure. Diamonds made in this way are not thought to be as beautiful as natural diamonds, but they are just as hard so can be used in industry.

After they are mined, diamonds are cut and polished to bring out the beauty of the gems.

Word bank   buckyball   short for buckminsterfullerene; hollow sphere of 60 carbon atoms

Graphite

Another form of carbon is graphite. Unlike diamond, graphite has a low density. The carbon atoms in graphite are joined together in layers, like pages in a book. The layers are not held together very strongly. This allows the layers to slide over each other. So graphite feels soft and slippery. Graphite is used as a **lubricant** in places such as the tracks of sliding doors.

Coal

Coal is a **mixture** of carbon and compounds that contain carbon and hydrogen. It is an important source of energy for factories and homes. Hard coal contains about 80 per cent carbon by **mass**. Soft coal contains about 40 to 50 per cent carbon. When coal is heated without air, the other compounds burn off leaving a form of carbon called coke. Coke is used to make iron and steel.

Buckyballs

In 1985 a new form of carbon was discovered in England. In the new form, 60 carbon atoms are arranged in a way that makes them look like a football. These forms of carbon became known as **buckyballs**. Buckyballs were named after Buckminster Fuller, a man who built domes with interlocking pieces.

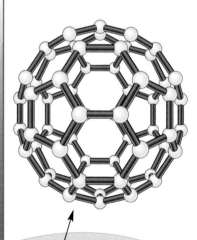

This diagram shows how carbon atoms are joined in a buckyball molecule. Scientists are still trying to find ways to use buckyballs.

Fast fact
The largest diamond ever found is called the Cullinan diamond. Its mass is 0.6 kilograms. That is about as much as a dozen eggs.

lubricant   slippery substance used to make machine parts move smoothly and easily

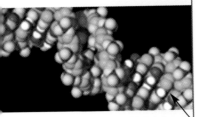

DNA is a chemical found in all our body cells. The small units in the drawing are groups of atoms. They contain carbon, hydrogen, nitrogen and phosphorus. The order in which the units are lined up is a code. Your cells use the code to make new cells. Every person has a unique DNA code.

Carbon in living things

Carbon compounds in living things are called **organic compounds**. In animals **proteins** make up cartilage, tendons and other body tissues. Proteins are long chains of smaller organic compounds. DNA is a code telling our body how to put these compounds together in the right order. For our bodies to make proteins, we must eat and digest proteins from foods. Meat, fish and dairy products are good sources of protein.

Blood or hair at a crime scene can be tested for DNA. This can help police find the person who committed the crime.

Carbohydrates are organic compounds of carbon, hydrogen and oxygen. Starch and sugar are carbohydrates. Fruits, vegetables and pasta contain starch and sugar and are good sources of the carbohydrates our bodies need for energy.

Woolly mammoths once roamed the northern parts of Europe, Asia and North America. Carbon dating revealed that one fossil mammoth from Canada died about 30,000 years ago.

carbohydrate   compound that contains carbon, hydrogen and oxygen
fossil   hardened remains of an ancient plant or animal

Cooking oils, fat in meat, and butter are examples of **lipids**. We need these compounds of carbon, hydrogen and oxygen to keep our cells working properly. But eating too many foods that contain lipids could be harmful.

Insect remains trapped in amber can be dated using carbon counts. This tells scientists whether the insect might have sucked dinosaur blood!

Carbon dating

Plants take in carbon in carbon dioxide. They use carbon dioxide to make their own food. Animals take in carbon by eating plants or other animals.

Some carbon **atoms** in living things change over time. This works a bit like an hourglass where sand grains pour one by one from the top to the bottom. In a similar way, the carbon atoms change one by one into different **elements**.

When a plant or animal dies, the number of these carbon atoms in its body starts to drop. Scientists can measure how much of this carbon is left in its body. So they can figure out how long ago the plant or animal died. This is called **carbon dating** and is one way scientists learn how old **fossils** are.

The dating game

Many things can be dated using carbon. They include:

- wood, twigs and seeds
- leather (animal skins)
- coprolites (fossilized animal dung)
- bone
- charcoal
- hair
- eggshells
- antlers and horns
- fish and insect remains
- seashells.

‹ ‹ ‹ ‹ ‹ ‹ ‹ ‹ ‹ ‹ ‹ ‹ ‹ ‹ ‹ ‹
Turn back to page 19 to find out how lipids like cholesterol can be harmful.

lipid   organic compound that includes fats and oils
organic compound   compound that contains carbon

The greenhouse effect

Burning fuels like coal helps to cause the **greenhouse effect**. The greenhouse effect is the warming of climates around the world. It is caused by an increase in the amount of carbon dioxide and other gases in the Earth's atmosphere.

Carbon dioxide traps heat radiating out from the Earth in the same way that glass traps heat in a greenhouse.

Carbon dioxide

All animals produce carbon dioxide when their cells use food. They give off this gas when they breathe out. Carbon dioxide also forms when carbon burns in air. When wood or other **fuels** burn, carbon in the fuel combines with oxygen in the air. The burning of **fossil fuels**, such as coal, natural gas and oil products, adds a lot of carbon dioxide to the air. Volcanoes also give off carbon dioxide.

Luckily, plants use carbon dioxide to make their own sugars. This helps to balance the carbon dioxide that is added to the air. However, cutting down forests means that less carbon dioxide is removed from the air. This allows carbon dioxide levels in the air to increase. More carbon dioxide in the air can change the Earth's climate.

Word bank   carbon monoxide   poisonous gas produced as carbon burns when there is not enough oxygen

Carbon monoxide

If carbon burns when there is not enough oxygen, it forms a gas called **carbon monoxide**. Carbon monoxide is a very **poisonous** gas. It keeps blood from carrying enough oxygen to body cells. Even a small amount of carbon monoxide can cause sleepiness and headaches. A gas fire or a car left running in a closed garage can produce enough carbon monoxide to kill someone.

Carbon monoxide detectors help save lives. A loud alarm lets people know if they are in danger. Homes should have carbon monoxide detectors on each floor. At least one should be located near the bedrooms. People who use portable heaters in tents or cabins can use battery-operated detectors.

Dry ice

When carbon dioxide is frozen at –78°C, it is called **dry ice**. It is a lot colder than ice made from water. It can be used to keep foods frozen when they are shipped. As it warms, it changes directly from a solid to gas.

Burning carbon-containing fuels like coal to produce electricity adds carbon dioxide to the air.

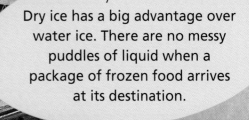

Dry ice has a big advantage over water ice. There are no messy puddles of liquid when a package of frozen food arrives at its destination.

dry ice   frozen carbon dioxide
fossil fuel   fuel found in the Earth, formed from dead organisms

Nitrogen

Air pollution

Nitrogen **oxides** form when nitrogen joins with oxygen. Car exhausts release nitrogen oxides into the air. They add to air pollution in many cities. Nitrogen dioxide can join with water in air to form nitric acid. The acid droplets fall to the Earth when it rains. This is called acid rain.

The air around us is made mostly of nitrogen. It makes up 78 per cent of the air we breathe. We take in large amounts of nitrogen every time we breathe. But we do not notice it because nitrogen has no colour, no **odour** and no taste.

Nitrogen is a **diatomic** gas, so the symbol for the gas is written as N_2 to show that its **atoms** are joined in pairs. Nitrogen gas does not react very easily with other **elements** or **compounds**. Even so, it still forms hundreds of thousands of compounds. These compounds are very important for industries, farming and living things. Some of these compounds also cause **pollution**.

Acid droplets can damage buildings, statues and living things.

Word bank   boiling point   temperature at which a liquid changes to a gas

Producing nitrogen

About 30 million tons of nitrogen gas are produced each year. Almost all of this is produced from air. Air is cooled to a very low temperature where it becomes liquid. Then it is slowly warmed. Each of the gases that make up air has a different **boiling point**. So as the air warms, each gas boils off separately. Nitrogen, which has a boiling point of about −196°C, is separated from the rest of the air and collected in tanks.

One of the uses of nitrogen gas is in the oil industry. Compressed nitrogen gas is pumped down oil wells. The pressure of the gas forces the oil upwards to the surface.

Airbags

Car airbags are made of thin nylon fabric that is folded into the steering wheel or dashboard. When a crash occurs, two nitrogen compounds react to produce nitrogen gas. Hot nitrogen gas fills the airbag faster than the blink of an eye.

The brownish haze seen over some cities is due to the presence of nitrogen dioxide in the air.

Nitrogen gas rushes into an airbag at up to 322 kilometres (200 miles) per hour.

Saving the apples

Fruit begins to go rotten mainly because it reacts with oxygen in the air. But nitrogen gas can be used to keep the picked fruit fresh. Apples can be stored for up to two years if they are kept at low temperatures in sealed rooms filled with nitrogen gas.

Nitrogen and living things

All living things need many **compounds** that contain nitrogen. Nitrogen occurs in many forms. But most living things cannot use nitrogen gas in air. Nitrogen is changed into usable compounds in two main ways.

- Some **bacteria** in soil and plant roots change nitrogen gas into nitrogen compounds. Plants use the nitrogen compounds to make **proteins**. When animals eat plants, they take in these plant proteins. Then the animals use them to make new proteins.

- When lightning passes through the air, it changes nitrogen gas to nitrogen compounds. These nitrogen compounds combine with rain water and form new compounds that plants can take in and use.

When dead animals and plants **decay**, simple nitrogen compounds form. Bacteria change some of these compounds back into nitrogen gas. The gas returns to the air. This movement of nitrogen is called the **nitrogen cycle**.

Nitrogen cycles through the living and non-living parts of the world.

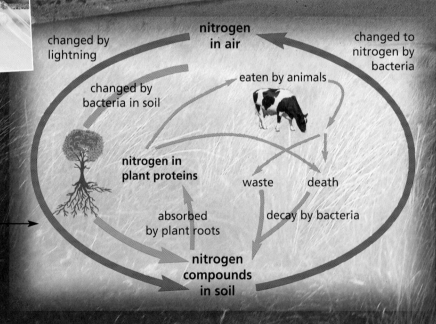

changed by lightning

changed to nitrogen by bacteria

changed by bacteria in soil

eaten by animals

nitrogen in air

nitrogen in plant proteins

waste   death

absorbed by plant roots

decay by bacteria

nitrogen compounds in soil

Word bank   decay   rot
bacteria   tiny living things too small to be seen except with a microscope

Uses of nitrogen

Modern farming often uses up most of the nitrogen compounds found in soil. So **fertilizers** are added to the soil. Many fertilizers are made from ammonia, a compound of nitrogen and hydrogen made using the Haber process.

Another important use of nitrogen is in making nitric acid. Nitric acid is a compound of hydrogen, nitrogen and oxygen. It is used to make fertilizers and explosives such as dynamite. It is also used to make nylon and other plastics.

Other nitrogen compounds are added to some canned and other preserved foods. They help stop the growth of harmful bacteria in the foods. Dentists use nitrous **oxide**, better known as 'laughing gas'. The sweet-smelling gas helps make patients more relaxed and the treatment less painful.

Liquid nitrogen

Nitrogen becomes a liquid at −196°C. That is very cold. A rubber ball placed in liquid nitrogen for just a few seconds becomes very **brittle**. If you tried to bounce it, it would shatter like glass into tiny pieces.

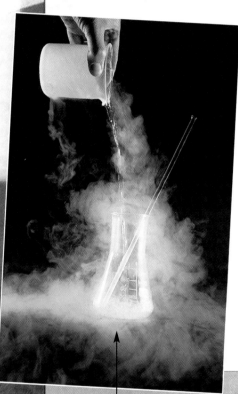

As liquid nitrogen is poured, its cold temperature condenses water vapour from the air around it.

> > > > > > > > > > > > >
Turn to pages 30 and 31 to find out how other non-metals cycle through our world.

nitrogen cycle   circular pathway in which nitrogen moves through the world

Oxygen

Fruit flies

Just a few minutes after being sliced, apples turn brown. This is because oxygen in the air combines with the fruit. Now scientists may have a new way to prevent this. They hope to make a spray from a **protein** found in houseflies that would stop chopped fruit from turning brown. Yum!

Properties and uses of oxygen

Oxygen is a **diatomic** gas with no colour, no **odour** and no taste. It makes up 21 per cent of the air. We make most oxygen from air. Air is cooled until it becomes liquid. Then it is slowly warmed. The other main parts of air – nitrogen and argon – boil off first. This leaves oxygen. Most oxygen is used as a compressed gas.

Importance of oxygen

People need oxygen gas to live. **Fuels** like oil and gas need oxygen to burn. So your home could not be heated without oxygen. Cars and buses could not run. You might think it would be better if there were more oxygen in the air. However, with more oxygen, things would burn more easily and quickly. That could be dangerous.

A fruit preservative made from powdered houseflies would be much cheaper than chemical preservatives.

Plants release oxygen into the air and absorb the carbon dioxide that animals breathe out.

Word bank photosynthesis process by which green plants use sunlight, water and carbon dioxide to make their own food

Oxygen and living things

Each time you breathe, you take in oxygen and breathe out some carbon dioxide. Plants take in carbon dioxide from the air. They release oxygen into the air.

Living things use much of the oxygen that is given off by plants during **respiration**. In respiration, sugars combine with oxygen. This process releases the energy that living things need. It also produces carbon dioxide and other products. Animals breathe out the carbon dioxide they produce. Plants release some of the carbon dioxide they produce during respiration through their leaves and other plant parts.

Fast fact
Without oxygen, a person could live for only about five minutes.

Most of the oxygen in the air comes from plants.

Food factories

Plants make their own food using a process called **photosynthesis**. They make food from carbon dioxide gas in the air and from water that their roots take from the ground. Plants use energy from sunlight to change the carbon dioxide and water into sugars and oxygen.

---

respiration   process in which a living thing takes in oxygen and uses it to produce energy, giving off carbon dioxide

Aeroplane emergency

Sodium chlorate is a compound of sodium, chlorine and oxygen. On aeroplanes, small containers of sodium chlorate and iron are above every seat. If oxygen is needed, a device sets off a small explosion that mixes the two chemicals. Oxygen gas is produced.

Oxygen masks drop down and let people breathe if the oxygen level drops in an aeroplane.

Fast fact

When things burn in air, oxygen is being used up. All fires need **fuel**, oxygen and heat to burn.

Oxygen compounds

Oxygen combines with almost every **element**. So there are far too many oxygen **compounds** to describe. Water is the most important oxygen compound. It is a compound of oxygen and hydrogen. It is one of the most common compounds on the Earth.

Oxygen makes up nearly half of the Earth's **crust**. It is found in many rocks and **minerals** in the Earth's crust. The most common oxygen compounds in the Earth's crust are oxides. An **oxide** is a compound of oxygen and another element. Many oxides, such as iron oxide, are **ores** from which we get important metals.

Oxygen also forms oxides that are gases. These include carbon dioxide and several nitrogen oxides.

Ozone

Oxygen also exists as a **triatomic** gas called **ozone**, O_3. Unlike ordinary oxygen, ozone has a faintly blue colour. It also has a strong **odour**. Ozone can be produced by electricity passing through air. People sometimes notice it during storms with lightning. They might also notice it around electrical motors in underground and railway stations.

Word bank ore   metal that is found combined with other elements
ozone   form of oxygen made of three oxygen atoms joined together

There is a layer of ozone in the upper part of the Earth's **atmosphere**. This ozone protects the Earth's surface from the harmful rays of the Sun. These rays can cause sunburn and skin cancer. Without the ozone layer, most living things on the Earth would be killed. In recent years, scientists have been concerned because the ozone layer is being destroyed. Chemicals that people release into the air are causing this problem.

The colours in this satellite photo show where ozone is present in the atmosphere. The dark area over the South Pole shows where ozone has been destroyed.

One way to avoid breathing in ozone is to wear a face mask.

Bad ozone

Ozone is not always helpful. Ozone is given off by car exhausts. Near the ground, ozone is a **pollutant**. It can harm people's lungs when they breathe it. Older people and children should not exercise outdoors when there is a lot of ozone in the air.

pollutant   harmful substance in the air, water or land
triatomic   three atoms of the same element joined together

Phosphorus and sulphur

Safety matches

The striking surface on a book of safety matches is made from a **mixture** of red phosphorus and powdered glass. When the head of a match is rubbed across it, some red phosphorus changes to white phosphorus. The white phosphorus bursts into flame and makes the match stick burn.

Matches used to be made of white phosphorus. Not only was this **toxic**, it easily burst into flame if the match box was shaken or left in sunlight.

Phosphorus

Phosphorus exists in three different forms. White phosphorus is a pale, waxy solid. Red phosphorus is a dark reddish powder. Black phosphorus is a flaky solid that forms when white phosphorus is put under high pressure. Below 35 °C, white phosphorus reacts with oxygen in the air and begins to glow. But if the air temperature is above 35 °C, white phosphorus bursts into flames and is converted to red phosphorus. Red phosphorus is much less active.

All living things need phosphorus. It is in all DNA and in our bones and teeth. About 20 per cent of the human skeleton is made of calcium phosphate. A phosphate is a **compound** of phosphorus, oxygen and another **element**. Most phosphorus is found in the form of phosphate rock. Phosphorus from this rock is used in making **fertilizers** for crops. Plants need phosphorus to grow.

Phosphorus

Highly Flammable   Toxic

White phosphorus must be stored in water to keep it from reacting with oxygen in the air. Red phosphorus is much more stable.

Word bank   geyser   hot water and steam underground that shoot up into the air every so often
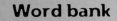

Sulphur

Sulphur is a brittle, yellow solid. It is often found at the edges of volcanoes and around the edges of some hot springs and **geysers**. Sulphur burns with a blue flame. Underground deposits of sulphur are found in Texas and Louisiana in the USA and in Mexico and Poland.

Sulphur and its compounds are used in fireworks, explosives, paints, plastics and dyes. Sulphur dioxide is used to keep some foods from rotting. It is also used as a bleach for cloth and for **wood pulp** used in making paper.

Most sulphur is used to make sulphuric acid. Sulphuric acid is used to make fertilizers and to remove rust from iron metal parts. It is also used in car batteries.

Sulphur in space

Sulphur is often found near volcanoes. Gases from volcanoes contain hydrogen sulphide and sulphur dioxide. These gases react to form the element sulphur.

One of Jupiter's moons, Io, has active volcanoes. It appears yellow in places because of sulphur deposits from its volcanoes.

Fast fact
- The old English name for sulphur was brimstone, which means 'a stone that burns'.
- Burning fuels that contain sulphur produces sulphur dioxide. This is one cause of acid rain.

toxic   poisonous
wood pulp   chipped wood with chemicals added, used to make paper

Halogens

Saving teeth

In some communities, small amounts of sodium fluoride are added to drinking water. This compound helps prevent tooth **decay** by making teeth stronger. Fluorides are also added to many toothpastes.

Brushing with fluoride toothpaste helps keep teeth healthy.

The halogens are the **elements** found in Group 7 of the **periodic table**. They are all non-metals with very similar properties. They have many uses in industry.

Fluorine

Fluorine is a pale yellow, **diatomic** gas. Two of its **atoms** are joined together. But it is much too active to be found in nature as a pure element. Because it is active, it reacts with other elements to form **compounds** called fluorides. Most fluorine is found in **minerals** in the Earth's **crust**. These minerals include fluorite and cryolite. Small amounts of fluorine are also found in sea-water, teeth, bones and blood.

Fluorine gas is used in preparing the uranium that is used in the nuclear reactors of power plants. Another use of fluorine is in making the non-stick surfaces of frying pans. The same fluoride is also used to make artificial valves for the heart.

Because chlorine in a water solution kills bacteria, it is used to treat swimming pools.

Word bank   mineral   non-living solid material from the Earth

Chlorine

Chlorine is a **poisonous**, yellowish-green diatomic gas. Its name comes from the Greek word *chloros*, meaning 'greenish-yellow'. In nature, chlorine mostly occurs in **dissolved** salts in sea-water and in the deposits in salt mines.

The smell near swimming pools is the **odour** of chlorine. Chlorine compounds are used to kill **bacteria** in the pool water. For the same reason, it is used to treat city water supplies and sewage. Household bleaches used to wash clothes contain chlorine compounds. Industries also use chlorine bleaches to whiten flour and paper. Another important use of chlorine is in making PVC plastic. This plastic is used to make many products including floor coverings, bicycle seats, garden hoses and pipes.

Gas attacks

Chlorine was used in Europe during World War I as a poison gas. Soldiers protected themselves from the gas by soaking cloth in urine and tying it around their noses and mouths. The ammonia in urine reacted with the chlorine and made it safe.

Three months after the first chlorine gas attack, World War 1 soldiers were given gas masks.

Preventing fires

Some compounds of bromine help prevent fires and slow the spread of fires. These compounds, called BFRs, are used in the plastic housings for TV sets and computer monitors. They are also used in fabric coverings for furniture and mattresses.

Iodine

Iodine is a shiny, greyish-violet solid at room temperature. It changes directly to a violet gas when heated. Iodine is **poisonous**. It is found in seaweed, in deep wells with salty water and in some **minerals**. Iodine **compounds** are called iodides.

Because iodine kills **bacteria**, campers often treat water with iodine tablets to make it safe to drink.

Bromine has a wide range of uses, including dyes, medicines, pesticides and photography.

Word bank   pesticide   chemical used to kill harmful insects or animals
radioactive   giving off particles or rays and changing to a different element

Iodine is needed to make the **thyroid** gland work properly. Small amounts of sodium iodide are sometimes added to table salt to make sure that people get enough iodine. Sodium iodide is also added to animal feeds in some places. Iodine mixed in alcohol is sometimes used to kill germs on cuts and scrapes. Silver iodide is used in making film for cameras. It can also be added to clouds to make them produce rain faster. This is expensive, but it might help to prevent droughts.

Bromine

Bromine is a reddish liquid that produces thick, reddish-brown fumes when exposed to air. Bromine is one of only two **elements** that are liquids at room temperature. The other one is the metal mercury. Bromine has a sharp, stinging **odour**. It is very poisonous and can burn the skin. Breathing its fumes can damage the linings of the nose and throat.

Bromine was discovered to be a new element in 1826 by a young French student. Its name comes from the Greek word bromos meaning 'stench' or 'bad smell'. Bromine is found in sea-water, in underground salt mines and in deep wells of salty water. Its compounds are called bromides. Their main uses are in making black-and-white film and in **pesticides**.

Astatine

Astatine is a very rare element and almost impossible to find in nature. Very little is known about it except that it is **radioactive**. Its name comes from the Greek word astatos, which means 'unstable'.

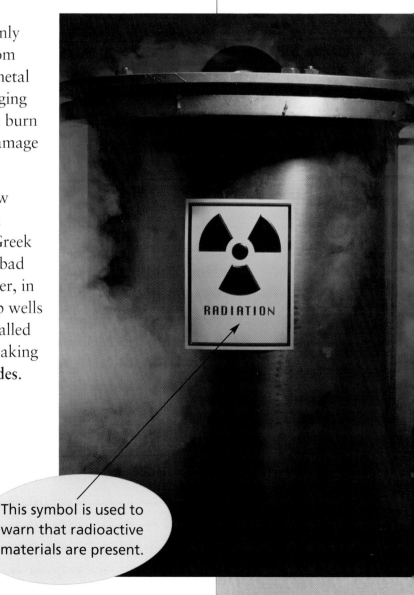

RADIATION

This symbol is used to warn that radioactive materials are present.

Fast fact

Some newer cars have halogen headlights. The bulbs in these lights contain small amounts of bromine or iodine, which makes the lights very bright.

thyroid gland in the neck that affects children's growth and affects how we all use food for energy

Noble gases

Breathing heliox

Divers working at high pressures underwater often breathe a **mixture** of helium and oxygen to avoid getting the bends. The helium replaces nitrogen in air, which would **dissolve** into the blood at high pressure. Breathing the heliox mixture makes divers' voices sound strange. Helium makes the divers' vocal cords vibrate faster. So their voices are higher in pitch.

The noble gases are on the far right side of the **periodic table**. All the gases in this group are colourless and **odourless**. They are called noble gases because they do not combine with other **elements** very often.

Helium

There is a lot of helium in the universe, but there's not very much on the Earth. In fact, helium was discovered on the Sun before it was discovered on the Earth. Its name comes from the Greek word *helios*, which means 'Sun'. On the Earth, most helium is found in natural gas.

Helium is less dense than air. That means it has a smaller **mass** than an equal **volume** of air does. So it is great for all kinds of balloons, from party balloons to airships. Scientists also use balloons filled with helium to study and measure conditions high in the **atmosphere**.

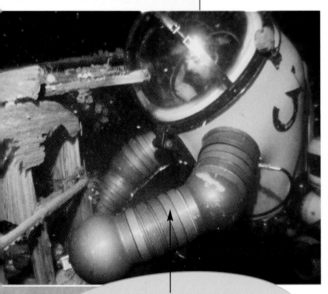

Deep sea divers breathe a mixture of 80 per cent helium and 20 per cent oxygen.

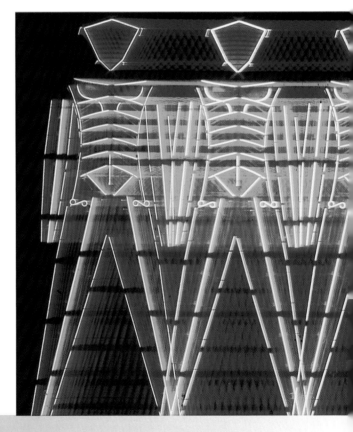

Neon

Neon is the fifth most common gas in the air. It forms no known **compound** with any other element. Neon is used along with helium in laser scanners. These kinds of scanners are used at the check-outs in supermarkets. They read the bar codes on food labels and enter the prices. Neon is also used in advertising signs. When electricity is passed through a tube filled with neon gas, the gas gives off an orange-red light.

Argon

Argon is the third most common gas in the air. It makes up almost one per cent of the air. Light bulbs are filled with argon instead of air. In advertising signs, argon gives off a purple light. Only one compound of argon is known. It is a compound of hydrogen, argon and fluorine.

A bright idea

Argon inside light bulbs will not react with the metal filament in the light bulb like oxygen in air would. This makes the filament, and the bulb, last longer. It also keeps the inside of the light bulb from turning dark.

Light bulbs do not glow purple because the argon in them is not hot enough.

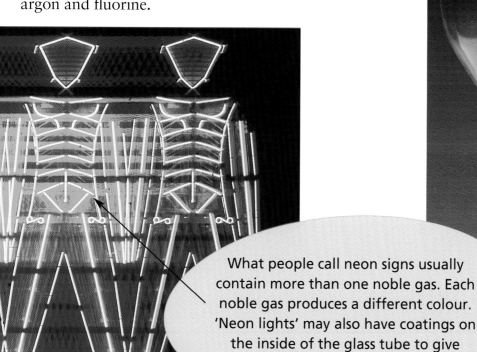

What people call neon signs usually contain more than one noble gas. Each noble gas produces a different colour. 'Neon lights' may also have coatings on the inside of the glass tube to give different coloured light.

A few compounds

In 1962, Neil Bartlett of the University of British Columbia made the first compound of a noble gas. The yellow-orange solid is a compound of xenon, platinum and fluorine. Since then tiny amounts of compounds of krypton, radon and argon have also been made.

In the 1960s, scientists at the Argonne National Laboratory near Chicago created several compounds of xenon.

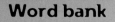

Krypton

The Earth's **atmosphere** contains one part krypton gas in every 900,000 parts of air. Krypton is used along with argon in some **fluorescent lamps**. It is also used in some flash lamps for high-speed photography. Krypton lights are also used to light landing strips at airports. When electricity is passed through a glass tube containing krypton, a bluish-violet light is given off. Using krypton in lights makes them brighter.

Until the 1960s, no **compounds** of krypton were known. Then krypton was found to react with fluorine to form a compound. But only a few grams of it have been made. Tiny amounts of a few other krypton compounds have also been made.

Word bank   fluorescent lamp   electric lamp made out of a tube coated with a powder that glows when electricity is passed through

Xenon

Xenon only exists in the air in very tiny amounts. But the gas can be separated from the air. Like the other noble gases, it is used in lighting displays. It gives off a bright, white light. It is also sometimes mixed with krypton and used in photographic flash bulbs.

Radon

Radon is a **radioactive** gas. If it is inhaled it can damage a person's lungs. Radon sometimes seeps into homes from the ground. People living in these homes can get lung cancer if the radon builds up to dangerous levels. Because it damages cells, radon has also been used to treat cancer. It is first pumped into tiny glass vials, called 'seeds'. The seeds are placed in a person's cancer **tumour**. **Radiation** from the radon kills the cancer cells but is kept away from normal body cells.

Testing for radon

Test kits are used to find out if a home has a radon problem. They stay in the home for between two and ninety days. Then the kit is sealed and sent to a lab. Results come back in a few weeks. Homes with radon problems can be fixed.

As uranium **decays**, radon gas is produced. This radon monitor is used in homes built on rocks that contain uranium.

Xenon is used in **strobe lights** where short flashes of light are needed for high-speed photography like sports or action shots.

radiation   rays and particles given off by a radioactive element
tumour   growth of body cells that is not normal and causes a swelling

Find out more

Organizations

The Royal Institute of Great Britain: Inside Out

Science information and resources for young people. Includes quizzes, amazing facts, discussion forums and games.
insideout.rigb.org

New Scientist

Magazine and website with all the latest developments in technology and science. Includes web links for young people.
newscientist.com

BBC Science

News, features and activities on all aspects of science.
bbc.co.uk/science

Books

Materials All Around Us, Robert Snedden (Heinemann Library, 2001)

Material World: Materials Technology, Robert Snedden (Heinemann Library, 2001)

Oxygen, Jean F. Blashfield (Raintree, 1999)

Science Files: Glass, Plastics Steve Parker (Heinemann Library, 2001)

World Wide Web

If you want to find out more about **non-metals**, you can search the Internet using keywords like these:

- non-metals + discovery
- 'Henry Cavendish'
- carbon + uses
- radon + UK
- Daniel Rutherford
- [name of a non-metal] + properties
- elements + 'periodic table'
- non-metals + KS3

You can also find your own keywords by using headings or words from this book. Use the search tips opposite to help you find the most useful websites.

Search tips

There are billions of pages on the Internet so it can be difficult to find exactly what you are looking for. For example, if you just type in 'water' on a search engine like Google, you'll get a list of 19 million web pages. These search skills will help you find useful websites more quickly:

- Know exactly what you want to find out about first
- Use simple keywords instead of whole sentences
- Use two to six keywords in a search, putting the most important words first
- Be precise – only use names of people, places or things
- If you want to find words that go together, put quote marks around them, for example 'periodic table' or 'transition metals'
- Use the advanced section of your search engine
- Use the + sign to add certain words, for example typing + KS3 into the search box will help you find web pages at the right level.

Where to search

Search engine

A search engine looks through the entire web and lists all the sites that match the words in the search box. They can give thousands of links, but the best matches are at the top of the list, on the first page. Try **bbc.co.uk/search**

Search directory

A search directory is more like a library of websites that have been sorted by a person instead of a computer. You can search by keyword or subject and browse through the different sites like you would look through books on a library shelf. A good example is **yahooligans.com**

Glossary

atmosphere layer of gases that surround the Earth

atom particles that make up all substances

bacteria tiny living things too small to be seen except with a microscope

boiling point temperature at which a liquid changes to a gas

brittle having a firm texture, but easily broken

carbohydrate organic compound that contains carbon, hydrogen and oxygen

carbon dating method of working out how long ago a plant or animal died by measuring the amount of a kind of carbon left in its body

carbon monoxide poisonous gas produced as carbon burns when there is not enough oxygen

chemical reaction change that produces one or more new substances

cholesterol fatty substance in some foods that can clog blood vessels

coke form of carbon made from coal

compound substance made of different kinds of elements joined together

compressed squeezed into a smaller space

conductor materials through which heat or electricity passes easily

crust outer layer of the Earth that we live on

decay rot

density mass of a certain volume of something; measured in grams per cubic centimetre or kilograms per cubic metre

diatomic when atoms of an element are found in pairs

dissolve mix completely and evenly

dry ice frozen carbon dioxide

ductile able to be drawn into wire

electron tiny, negatively charged particle outside the nucleus of an atom

element substance made of only one kind of atom

fertilizer chemicals added to soil to help plants grow better

flammable easily set on fire

fluorescent lamp electric lamp made of a tube coated with a powder that glows

fossil hardened remains of an ancient plant or animal

fossil fuel fuel found in the Earth's rocks, formed from ancient plant and animal life

fuel any material that can be burned to produce useful heat or power

geyser hot water and steam underground that shoot up into the air every so often

graphite a form of carbon, used in pencils

greenhouse effect warming of the Earth's climate caused by an increase in carbon dioxide in the air

insulator material through which heat or electricity does not pass easily

ion atom or group of atoms that has an electric charge

lipid organic compound that includes fats and oils

lubricant slippery substance used to make machine parts move smoothly and easily

lustre shine that metals have

malleable able to be hammered, rolled or shaped without breaking

mass amount of matter that makes something up; measured in grams or kilograms

metalloids elements that have properties of both metals and non-metals

mineral non-living solid material from the Earth

mixture two or more substances that are placed together, but not joined

neutron uncharged particle in the nucleus of an atom

nitrogen cycle circular pathway in which nitrogen moves through the world

nucleus dense, positively charged centre of an atom

odour smell

opaque not letting light pass through

ore metal that is found combined with other elements

organic compound compound that contains carbon

oxide compound of oxygen and another element

ozone form of oxygen made of three oxygen atoms joined together

periodic table chart in which elements are arranged in groups according to similar properties

pesticide chemical used to kill harmful insects or animals

photosynthesis process by which green plants use sunlight, water and carbon dioxide to make their own food

poisonous having a dangerous or harmful effect

pollutant harmful substance in the air, water or land

pollution harmful things in the air, water or land

protein organic compound that contains nitrogen and is built up of amino acids

proton positively charged particle in the nucleus of an atom

radiation rays and particles given off by a radioactive element

radioactive giving off particles or rays and changing to a different element

respiration process in which a living thing takes in oxygen and uses it to produce energy, giving off carbon dioxide

strobe light very bright light that can flash thousands of times each second

synthetic man-made

thyroid gland in the neck that affects children's growth and affects how we all use food for energy

translucent stopping some, but not all, light from passing through

transparent letting light pass through

triatomic three atoms of the same element joined together

tumour a growth of body cells that is not normal and causes a swelling

volume amount of space something takes up

wood pulp chipped wood with chemicals added; used to make paper

Index

Raintree freestyle Curriculum version

Series in the *Freestyle Curriculum Strand* include:

Turbulent Planet

Energy Essentials

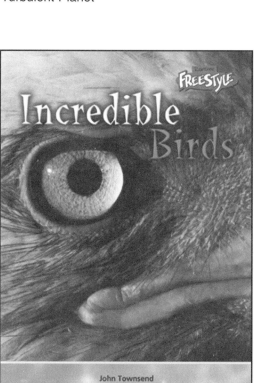

Incredible Creatures

Material Matters

Find out about the other titles in these series on our website www.raintreepublishers.co.uk